Fry to Sea Horse

Camilla de la Bédoyère

QEB Publishing

L2
j597.67
De la Bedoyere

Words in **bold** are explained in the Glossary on page 22.

Copyright © QEB Publishing, Inc. 2010

Published in the United States by
QEB Publishing, Inc.
3 Wrigley, Suite A
Irvine, CA 92618

www.qed-publishing.co.uk

All rights reserved. No part of this publication may be reproduced, stored in a retrieval system, or transmitted in any form or by any means, electronic, mechanical, photocopying, recording, or otherwise, without the prior permission of the publisher, nor be otherwise circulated in any form of binding or cover other than that in which it is published and without a similar condition being imposed on the subsequent purchaser.

A CIP record for this book is available from the Library of Congress.

ISBN 978 1 60992 049 4

Printed in the United States

Editor Alexandra Koken
Designer and Picture Researcher Melissa Alaverdy

Picture credits
(t=top, b=bottom, l=left, r=right, c=center)

Alamy 1b Wolfgang Poelzer, 6t Papilio, 16-17 Juniors Bildarchiv, 17t blickwinkel

Corbis 18-19 Specialist Stock

Getty 6b Georg Grall/National Geograpic, 14 Science Faction, 16 Chris Newbert

OceanwideImages.com 1t, 10, 11t, 13b, 13t, 14-15, 21t Rudie Kuiter, 5c, 5t Gary Bell, 20-21 Michael Patrick O'Neill

Photolibrary 4 LOOK-foto, 7 Douwna Georgette, 8-9 Oxford Scientific, 11c Peter Arnold Images, 12 Oxford Scientific, 18 Max Gibbs, 19 Waterframe Underwater Images, 20b Tips Italia, 22 Peter Arnold Images, 24 LOOK-foto

Shutterstock front cover Studio 37, back cover Ryhor M Zasinets, 2t Koshevnyk, 2 Chen Wei Seng, 3t angel digital, 24 Koshevnyk

Contents

What is a Sea Horse?

A sea horse is a type of fish. It has **scales**, a tail, and **fins**.

Fish live underwater. They can live underwater because they have **gills**. They use gills to breathe.

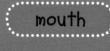

fin

mouth

Sea horses live in the sea. They do not look like most fish.

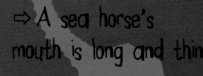

⇨ A sea horse's mouth is long and thin.

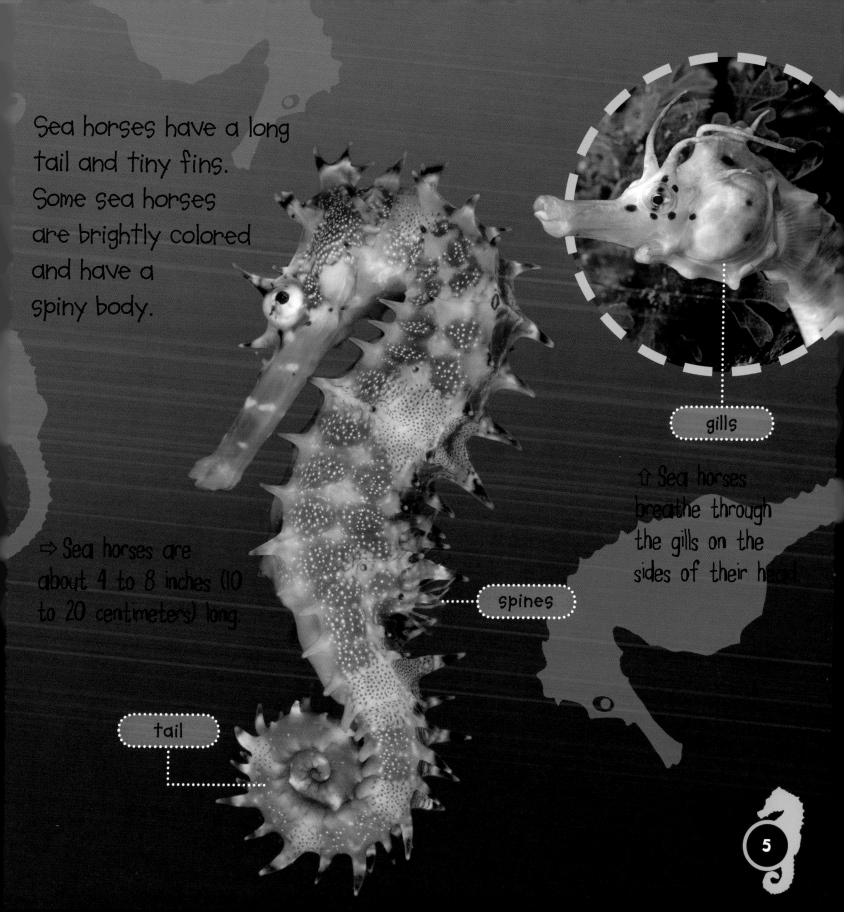

Sea horses have a long tail and tiny fins. Some sea horses are brightly colored and have a spiny body.

⇨ Sea horses are about 4 to 8 inches (10 to 20 centimeters) long.

gills

⇧ Sea horses breathe through the gills on the sides of their head.

spines

tail

The Story of a Sea Horse

A baby sea horse is called a **fry**. All fry begin life as eggs, which are laid by their mother. Newborn fry are also called **hatchlings**.

Female sea horses lay the eggs and the males look after them.

2

fry

⇧ The fry look like their parents.

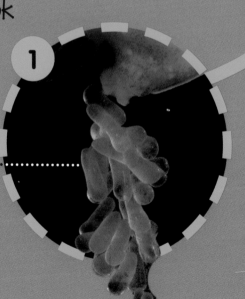

1

egg

⇦ The eggs of a sea horse are very small.

3

adult

The amazing story of how a tiny egg grows into a fry, and then into an adult sea horse, is called a **life cycle.**

⇨ When a sea horse is grown it is called an adult.

Time to Dance

Male and female sea horses come together to **mate**. Before they mate, the sea horses dance for each other.

male

Their special mating dance is called a **courtship**. The sea horses wrap their tails around each other, and swim together.

⇨ Male sea horses choose the biggest females to mate with.

female

Courtship dances
can happen every
day for a few
days, until the
female is ready
to lay her eggs.

Life Begins

A male sea horse has a special pouch on his belly. After dancing, the pouch gets bigger.

pouch

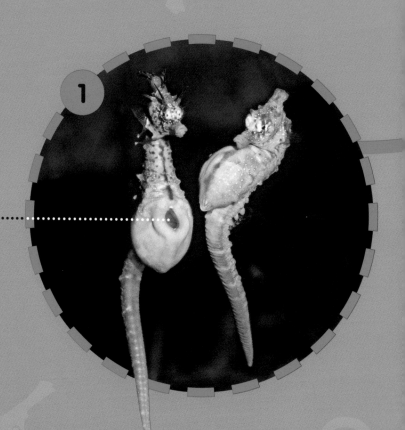

A female sea horse lays her eggs in the male's pouch. The male closes the pouch and seals it, so the eggs cannot float away. The male **fertilizes** the eggs inside his pouch.

⇧ The female carefully lays her eggs inside the male's pouch.

2

3

⇧ The male and female stay close together so that no eggs are lost.

⇨ The male sea horse now holds all the eggs. We say that he is pregnant.

Caring for the Eggs

The fertilized eggs stay in the male sea horse's pouch for up to six weeks. He looks after them carefully while they grow.

Each egg has food for the fry growing inside it. Some fry also get food from their father's body.

⇨ The pouches of these two pregnant males are filled with tiny fry.

Soon, the fry are ready to leave the pouch. As soon as the fry are born they swim away.

⇨ Some fry spend only two weeks in the pouch.

fry

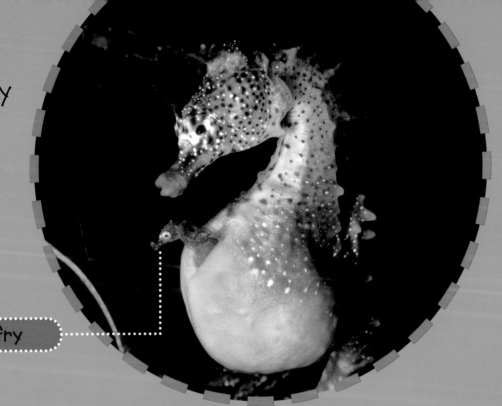

⇦ The male pushes the fry out from his pouch quickly.

Next Steps

Some sea horses give birth to just five fry at a time. Others can have hundreds.

The fry are too small to swim well. They wrap their tails around plants or **coral**. Some fry are carried away by the water.

⇧ Newborn fry suck tiny bits of food into their mouth.

⇩ A newborn fry
might be just
0.2 inches
(5 millimeters) long.

Growing Up

The hatchlings are very small when they are born. As they get older they grow bigger.

The fry have to look after themselves. Their parents do not look after them. Fry have to find food to eat, and hide from fish that want to eat them.

⇨ This hatchling will be an adult when it is about five months old.

They eat small sea animals such as brine shrimp.

When they become adults, the sea horses look for mates. The life cycle begins again.

⇦ This is a zebra-snout sea horse. It will be an adult when it is nine months old.

How Sea Horses Live

Sea horses are not good swimmers. They wrap their curly tail around plants, so the water does not drag them away.

Most sea horses have colors, patterns, or spines that help them to stay hidden, or **camouflaged**. Other sea animals want to eat them, so hiding is a good idea!

⇧Most sea horses live in warm, shallow water.

Sea horses eat other animals. They stay still, and grab any small animals that swim past.

⇦Leafy sea dragons can hide easily in seaweed and other plants.

⇩Sea horses suck up food through their snout.

19

Saving Sea Horses

Sea horses are amazing animals, and people like to see them.

In the past, many sea horses were taken from the sea and put in **aquariums**.

There are more than 30 types of sea horse, and most of them are very rare.

⇦ The best place to watch sea horses is in the wild.

Many people are trying to save sea horses for the future.

⇧ Sea horses may die out if people keep taking them from the sea.

⇦ This is a longnose sea horse. Like other sea horses, it is rare.

Glossary

Aquarium
A place where fish are kept.

Camouflage
Colors and patterns that help an animal to hide.

Coral
Stony shapes built by tiny sea animals.

Courtship
When males and females are planning to mate.

Fertilize
When a male fertlizes a female's egg, it can grow into a new living thing.

Fin
Part of a fish's body that it uses to swim.

Fry
A baby fish.

Gill
Part of a fish's body that is used to breathe.

Hatchlings
Fry that have just come out of their eggs.

Life cycle
The story of how a living thing grows and changes, and produces young.

Mate
When a male fertilizes a female's eggs the animals are mating.

Scale
Hard little pieces of skin that cover a fish's body.

Index

Notes for Parents and Teachers

Look through the book and talk about the pictures. Read the captions and ask questions about the things in the photographs that have not been mentioned.

Use the Internet* or books to discover the enormous variety of shapes, colors, and sizes of fish in the world's oceans and seas. Use a range of materials to create a large collage of some of the most colorful fish you find.

Enjoy imaginative play together. Encourage the child to pretend to be a parent animal—such as a father penguin or sea horse, or a mother hen or dog. Help the child to practice caring for, feeding, and protecting their young.

Talking about a child's family helps them to link life processes, such as growing and changing, to their own experiences. Drawing simple family trees, looking at photo albums, and sharing family stories with grandparents are fun ways to engage young children.

Be prepared for questions about human life cycles. There are plenty of books for this age group available that can help you give age-appropriate explanations. Talk about the way human parents prepare for the arrival of a baby, and how families share the task of looking after a newborn.

*The publishers cannot accept responsibility for information, links, or any other content of Internet sites, or third-party websites.

24

.